When bikes were invented, they had no pedals. The rider had to run along the road while sitting on the bike!

no pedals

These running bikes were sometimes called hobby horses or dandy horses.

This boneshaker bike was invented later. It was one of the early bikes with pedals.

pedals

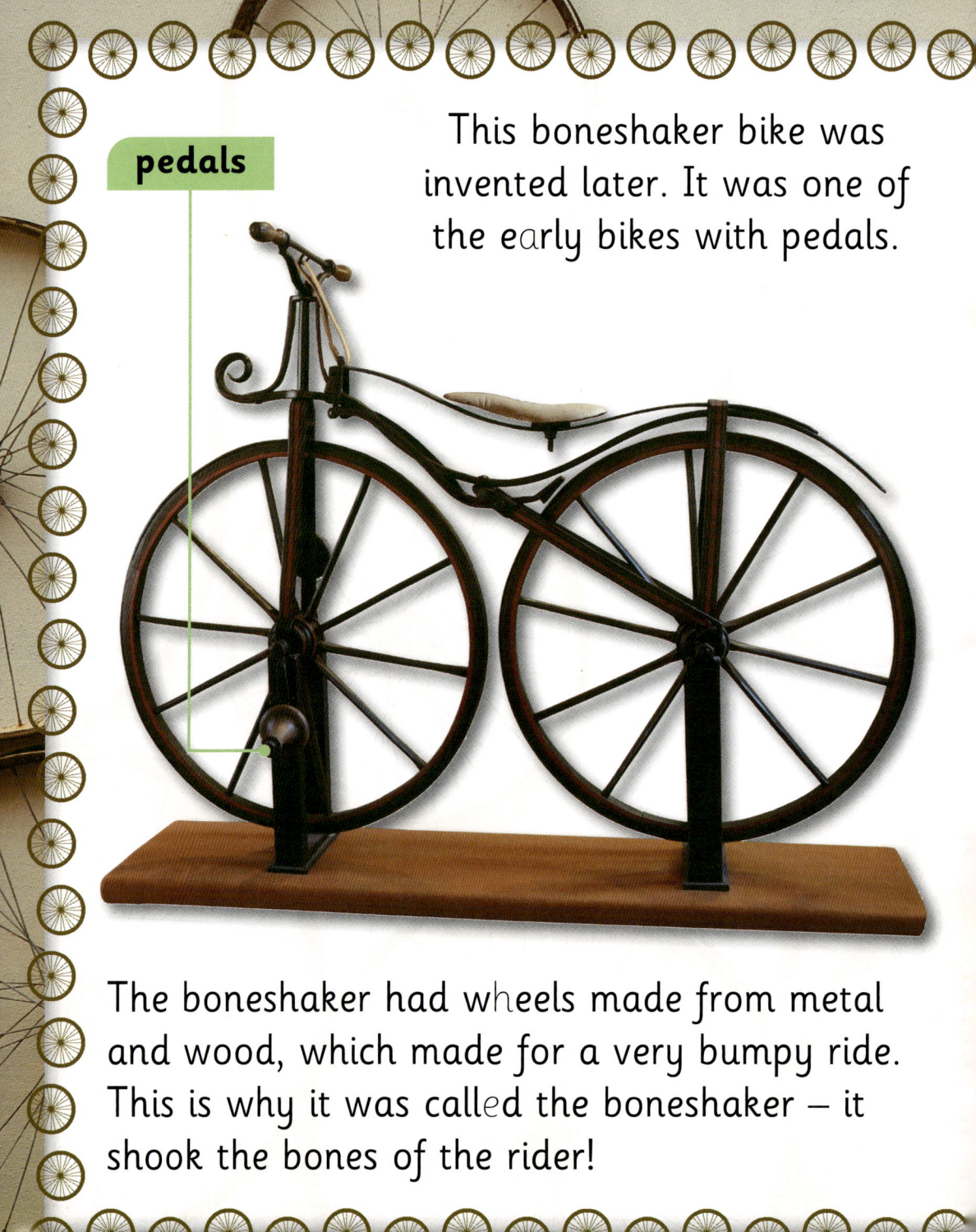

The boneshaker had wheels made from metal and wood, which made for a very bumpy ride. This is why it was called the boneshaker – it shook the bones of the rider!

This penny-farthing used to be a very common bike. Its pedals were in the middle of a big wheel, which made it quicker than the boneshaker.

pedals

big wheel

a penny

a farthing

The penny-farthing was named for a big coin called a penny and a small coin called a farthing. The different size coins looked like the different size wheels.

The penny-farthing was quick for its time, but it was not very safe.

You had to sit on top of the big wheel, quite far from the ground. It was common to hit your head or get your legs trapped if you fell off.

speedy, but unsafe

Penny-farthings are no longer ridden very much. Instead we have safer, more modern bikes.

Road bikes are speedy and safer.

The wheels of a modern bike are normally the same size.

Mountain bikes and road bikes look similar but they are not exactly the same.

Mountain bikes are built to go up mountains. They have thick wheels, which makes them grip the loose tracks better.

The handlebars on mountain bikes are straight.

Road bikes are built for speed. They have thin wheels and a thin frame, which make them go quicker.

Road bikes' handlebars are shaped like the letter 'c'.

BMX bikes have small wheels, which helps the riders to do tricks and stunts.

This rider is upside-down!

a rail

BMX riders use ramps and rails to do flips and jumps.

ramps

A trike is a bike with three wheels. Trikes are normally for young children, but you can get them for adults, too.

an adult on a trike

You can get bikes with four wheels as well!

Sometimes, children's bikes do not have pedals.

Toddler bikes like this are used to help young children learn to sit on and ride a proper bike.

Sitting steady on a bike is the hardest part!

Not all bikes are for one person. A tandem is a bike for two riders. Count the number of saddles, handlebars and pedals.

You can get triplet tandems for three riders, too!

These are the main parts of a bike.

Children's bikes sometimes have training wheels as well as big wheels.

saddle

frame

training wheels

pedal

What makes a bike go?

When you pedal on a bike, the chain goes around. This makes the wheels spin around, and this is what makes the bike go along. You do not have to pedal hard to go downhill.

pedals go around

chain goes around

wheels go around

bike goes along

What makes a bike stop?

If you need to stop, you squeeze the brakes. This makes the brake pads press against the rims of the wheels to stop them going around.

brake pad

wheel rim

Some bikes have disc brakes instead of brake pads.

Having brakes makes bikes safer.

a disc brake

Ride a bike safely with this checklist

1. Get a bike helmet.

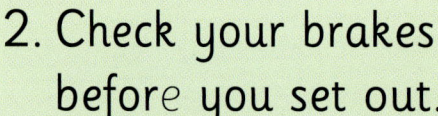

2. Check your brakes before you set out.

3. Pump up the wheels.

4. Sit on the saddle and check that your feet touch the ground.